Early Settlement and Other Poems

*Charlie Churchill*

# Early Settlement and Other Poems

Charles Churchill

Illustrated by Dawn Marion

Beech River Books
Center Ossipee, N.H.

**Copyright © 2006 by Charles Churchill**

All rights reserved. No part of this book may be reproduced or transmitted in any form by means, electronic or mechanical, including photocopying and recording, or by any information storage or retrieval, without written permission from the publisher, except for brief passages quoted by a reviewer in a newspaper or magazine.

BRB

Beech River Books
P.O. Box 62, Center Ossipee, N.H. 03814
1-888-874-6904
www.beechriverbooks.com

LIBRARY OF CONGRESS CATALOGING-IN-PUBLICATION DATA

Churchill, Charles, 1927-
Early settlement and other poems / Charles Churchill ; illustrated by Dawn Marion. -- 1st ed.
p. cm.
ISBN-13: 978-0-9776514-8-1 (pbk.)
ISBN-10: 0-9776514-8-7 (pbk.)
1. New England--Poetry. I. Marion, Dawn, 1953- II. Title.

PS3603.H885E24 2006
813'.6--dc22
2006029309

Illustrated by Dawn Marion

Printed in the United States of America

*To my grandmothers
and all the other
wonderful women in my life.*

## *Foreword*

Other poets I know write just about everyday. I do not, keeping the muse at a distance by fishing, hunting, visiting with friends, and volunteering for projects within my community. The poetry contained in this little book is much of what I have written from the early 1950s to the present time.

The Early Settlement poems represent my hardest work, my most consistent concentration. Where I live in the mountains of Porter, Maine, surrounded by old cellar holes, it is easy to see the working of the Industrial Revolution. Children, viewing the hardships endured by their parents, walked out to the towns, the mills, the social life. When their parents were no longer able to keep up their homes, they moved in with their children "down town."

## Contents

Part One

| | |
|---|---|
| Of Walls and Men | 3 |
| Midnight Apples | 4 |
| Counterclockwise Silent Time | 6 |
| Deer in Winter | 7 |
| Swamp Deer | 8 |
| Duck in Spring | 9 |
| Winter Dreams | 10 |
| Hawk | 11 |
| A Sound of Weeping | 12 |
| Vision | 15 |
| Forever | 16 |
| Bass Man | 17 |
| Sliding | 18 |
| Of Trees and Walls | 19 |
| Bob Sled | 20 |
| Ice-Out Day | 21 |
| Ice-Out Loons | 21 |
| The Bridge | 23 |
| Weather Report | 24 |
| Music | 25 |
| Ocean Eye | 26 |
| Planting | 27 |
| Song | 28 |
| Amy | 29 |
| Pathways | 31 |

| | |
|---|---|
| Smelting Time | 32 |
| Tides | 33 |

## Early Settlement

| | |
|---|---|
| Old Cellar | 37 |
| First Settlement | 39 |
| Ephraim | 41 |
| Andrew | 42 |
| Mary | 44 |
| Adam | 45 |
| Samuel | 47 |
| Clara | 49 |
| Eunice Foss | 50 |
| Angie Blake | 51 |
| Walter | 52 |
| Mill Town | 53 |
| Moving Day | 55 |
| Old Dog | 57 |
| Reclamation | 59 |

*Part One*

## *Of Walls and Men*

Stark monuments to toil, the old stone walls
Convey uncertain words from ancient deeds
And by their very width of rock proclaim
The strength of man's eternal will to own
What he can never hope to hold for long.

Some great-grandfather's younger eyes surveyed
This ponderous fruit of centuries that filled
His farm, and he and others bent their backs
To lift, to place in balance for a wall,
These scattered orphans from the glacier's womb.

You come across them deep in pines and oaks,
Mute sentinels that guard forgotten fields.
These solid links of hard necessity
Still seem a barrier set against the world,
A rural handiwork of ancient gods.

## Midnight Apples

When I look out through misty kitchen windows
And see my apple trees loom up, fruit heavy
In the grasp of early morning frost—fog air,
I sometimes think of those that stand a half mile
Down the road—behind my wall, beyond my view.
Each spring they blossom with the rest and summer sees
The tiny apples start to grow, until
By fall the trumpet frost rings out and leaves
Red echoes on the larger juicy globes.
Last night I stayed awake again to hear
The cars go by, and some I know went not
Too far before they stopped still by my wall.
What baskets fill beneath a stealthy braille
I never know for sure 'til picking time,
When I see my roadside trees stand straighter
Than all the rest beneath their lighter load.
Perhaps these folk think apple trees are theirs
And nature's own, but no, the good nature's mine,
For I could, if I wished, put up a logging chain
Between this darker deed and where they live.
I choose instead to lie awake at night
And wish these apple-bandit folks I hear
Pass by might come by day and ask me for
My bough-held store. It might well compensate
For sweat, spray, mulch and honey bees if I
Could see who took my fruit and heard them thank

Me for it. Perhaps by this they'd come to know
My views on life and, yes, on apples trees
And I could get a longer fall night's sleep.

## Counterclockwise Silent Time

When mares' tails swish pure white on winter sky,
I don't need a weather map or weather man
To tell me that a snow low's on the way.
They go from West to East and, oh, I hope
Each one, at least, will stay around our sky
Just long enough to dump two feet of snow
Upon a life that always moves too fast.
I'd like a day that knows no outward mark
Of mine, a precious lapse outside this world
That brings a closeness out of touch with time—
A day to be alone with those I love:
The tiny girl who never tires of hearing
Daddy read, the smaller son who tries so hard
To let me know he likes it just as much,
The wife who never has the time it seems
To stop a while and turn out decent fudge.
"Winters are not now what they used to be,"
My father's mother used to say. "They drove
Whole teams across the crust, and when it snowed,
We often knew a week-long comfort by the fire."
I sometimes think of all the things we've lost
To snow blowers, mammoth plows and endless salt.
The weekends with their lists of things to do
Seem only to extend the working week.
A mid-week snow storm, stark and deep, could bring
An honest slowness to a day, a time
For me that, somehow, always moves too fast.

*Deer in Winter*

Two months beyond the time when rifles, bows
And muskets found their racks, a winter day
I moved on nearly silent skis between
The sleeping earth and powder domes of pines.

As newer snowflakes fell, I sensed beneath
My feet a path that led me down to swamp,
And there I sudden saw a brush of white
On white, a motion out of touch with trees.

And then, much deeper than most men see, I saw
Within a mist of snow, stiff, huddled shapes
In coats of winter grey, heads down against
The day and pawing at the frozen earth.

I pulled my collar up against the cold.
It was enough, for when I looked again,
I saw stark trees and nothing else. It made
Me wonder if a winter day had shown me ghosts.

## Swamp Deer

"The deer went in the swamp. I'm sure of it,"
He said. But I could see he was a native
And, as such, perhaps knew better. So I walked
On up the ridges through the swirling, noisy
Oak leaves, and later on that morning, saw
And shot one of the deer "that went in the swamp."
I also saw the foot-of-the-mountain sage
Walking along quite fast and, yes, he tried
To act surprised at what I was dragging past.
"Well, sir," said he, "perhaps I was wrong in
Thinking they was down below. Maybe you
Can tell me, boy, just which way'd they go?"
"The deer went in the swamp. I'm sure of it," I said.

## Duck in Spring

"I guess he froze to death," he'd said and strung
The duck up high beside his ice house door,
A decoration for his winter time.
Through blizzards stark and deep and winter thaw
I saw its colors dim, a little more
Each day, and when the new spring currents forced
The house away, the duck was left behind.
I saw it next, a darkened lump, a foot
Or so from open bay, a mallard drake
With graying eyes, too rotten for the gulls.
I also saw his kin go glistening by,
Eating, mating, quackcophonous in spring,
And if they saw or cared, they gave no sign.
Perhaps they'd learned to deal with what was real.

*Winter Dreams*

Upon my lake the sound of
   boats has long since
Fled to winter hills,
   and there are dreams,
When silence blends
   with utter cold,
Consuming summer things
   that may have had
Some great or small
   significance upon my life.
In the morning, where the
   snow has blown away,
I see the cracks within
   the ice that
Start upon my shore and
   lead on down the lake,
And I hear once more
   the pounding cry
Of infant ice upon the
   temple hills.

## Hawk

A nephew of a man just down the road
Signed up to trade a weekend time each month
For extra cash to buy a better life
With benefits he could not live without,
As close to home I coaxed a chipmunk down
A tree with more than what he had before—
Black sunflower seeds—and offered in a hand
He came to trust a little more each day.
A time he did not come, then heard the news
Of war and saw a solitary hawk
High up, still hunting in my neighbor's tree.

## A Sound of Weeping

There you go! Will you sing? Will you dance? Will you run?
Will you show all the things you have made?
Take your turn on the slide? Can you climb up again?
Is it time for the circus parade?

Can you read? Can you spell? Can you add four and two?
Can you trace all the routes to the West?
Take your seat in the row at the back of the room;
It's time for your algebra test.

> So close to dawn on spring-lit days
> The children go on leaping,
> But far ahead, beyond their ears,
> There comes the sound of weeping.

The padded boys go thrusting by
While shapely girls lead cheers.
Hot rubber burns on moon-lit roads,
And cokes lose out to beers.

Then music of the night and stars
Is echoed in the blood,
And hearts that beat a solo part
Are swept away by flood.

There is, in later spring, a warmth
In secrets that are keeping,
But nearer now beyond the hills,
There comes the sound of weeping.

Mortgaged homes with struggling lawns
Have bright, new swings out back,
And parents inside paying bills
Who dwell on things they lack.

Braces build a better smile,
College kids by far do best,
And mother's got herself a job
That helps with all the rest.

The sun at noon is searing hot,
Then shadows start their creeping,
And faintly on a western breeze
There comes the sound of weeping.

Gone are the sounds of the younger folk,
Here for a weekend or two.
They all have children of their own
And all those things to do.

Pain is a page of the daily book.
Pills have their place near the bed,
And father with his crooked cane
Forgets the things he's said.

The sun moves on to western sky
Where dreams are not for keeping.
Within the mind where shadows steal,
There is the sound of weeping.

*Vision*

Last year I stayed inside one winter day
While blowing powder snow piled stark and deep
Against my drafty doors and window panes,
A day that knew no outward mark of mine.
I did not move too far and thought of life
Within the womb, without the world, and life
Beyond this world, where a multitude of eyes
Defy what little man has brought to light.

*Forever*

After separation and divorce
    we talked sometimes
Twice or more a month, and when
    you weren't at home,
There was your voice
    saying the same old things.
And when you went to hospice
    for your last two weeks on earth,
I heard the recording
    one more time
Before it was replaced by
    the telephone company's voice—
Cold, dispassionate, and I
    knew you were gone,
And the house was gone, and I cried
    for all that had gone.
I went by once after the
    "For Sale" sign had been
Replaced by somebody's wheelbarrow
    and saw new outside furniture on the deck.
And I thought again about forever
    and all it could not mean.

## Bass Man

His boat hung by its anchor in the rip tide,
A tiny watch being swung on its chain
By a laughing giant who could, if he wished,
Heave it to the heavens, scattering mainspring, gears,
And jewels into the depths around the stars.
But if he feared the force beneath his ancient hull,
He gave no sign. His movements, bought from the tides
With time, showed in their slowness that he knew
What could and could not be done with the sea.
He had one old rod and a plastic pail
And never once looked up to see the fancy
Fishing boats on their way to better spots.
And later on, when time and tide were done,
He shipped his anchor and left, fish-heavy
In the shadows of a Sunday afternoon.

*Sliding*

So long ago it seems another life,
We hauled our sleds uphill on solid crust,
Then flung ourselves on wood and steel and flew
Forever down the sun or moon-bright snow.
How far? Perhaps two hundred yards, no more.
What younger eyes had magnified now holds
The leveled graves of those who watched us slide,
The leveled graves of those who slid with us.
A year before he died, I saw the best
Of friends go walking back and forth between
A water spout and flowers placed upon
His lady's grave that day. I would have said
"Good morning," but could not find those simple words.
I doubt he saw the morning either good
Or ill, but only that it gave him time
To share what part of life he could
From what he knew was left. Because we cannot
Know what others think, I was left to wonder
If he thought of sleds and sliding on this hill.
Perhaps he knew and would not say, his world
And mine had lost the last best place to slide.

## *Of Trees and Walls*

The quiet, peering ones came first and left
Their little flags and painted trees to point
The way for great-wheeled things with throaty roar
And blades of steel that traveled in and out
To leave a path for trucks and helmet folk
With cables, cranes, and large and smaller saws.

New dawns led on to days and days of smoke
Of oil and gas and scream and snarl of saws,
Dull thud of dying trees. Tall hemlock, pine
And heavy oak were sawn to size and stacked
Five high or more on trucks, each chained-up load
Log-heavy hearse on highway out of town.

When all the limbs and stumps and roots were trucked,
They found a market eager for the walls,
Then took them, high and low, and stone by stone,
And left a jagged ditch where walls had been—
No longer any need for lines to show
The place of early fields, forgotten farms.

The peering, quiet ones came back and laid
Out lots and streets and water lines. Then signs
Went up and down, and newer homes were built
Just far enough apart to be too close.
My neighbor bought two little trees to plant
And built a wall between his place and mine.

## Bob Sled

When I was ten my father trucked it from
The farm, the largest sled I ever saw,
And told me, as he touched the wheel, how years
Ago his cousins and two neighbor boys
Would meet on winter nights to make one run
And make that ride suffice for winter fun.

One ride a night was all they could expect,
Six country boys who used what strength they had
To haul a sled of oak and steel up Merrill Hill,
Where burden come to briefest rest became
A sudden beast that hurled along at mile-
A-minute speed down steepest road in town.

My father wheeled and dealed and never kept
A thing for long, and so I never had
My ride with him. The sled? I think it may
Have come to rest in some museum place
Where tourists come to touch another's past,
A part of me I did not wish to leave.

*Ice-Out Day*

I took time off to watch the ice go out
The other day and lingered, longer than
I thought I would, to watch a newly-floated
Log bob here and there, as in the jaws of a wind
Unable to decide which side to chew.
At length it found the shore and a good old boy
With chain saw spewing golden chips who saw
At once the gift. "Damn sight better'n
What I got and all limbed out. Wet don't
Do no harm. Dry wood floats. Burn it all tonight."
Perhaps I tried too hard for message here.
There may be other logs to watch next year.

*Ice-Out Loons*

The loons always seem to arrive as soon
As the ice goes out. They cannot live on land
And so I must assume they hear a kind
Of loony weather report while dipping
For smelts on open water somewhere else.
Who knows? They're here as if they never left.

## The Bridge

Too far from town to rate repair—and yearly
More remote—the old stone bridge divides low
Pasture walls and midway sags from seasons'
Light or heavy loads that passed or lingered there.
Some weeks ago Dwight Mills recalled a deed
That said this bridge was more than just a bridge
But was, in truth, an overpass of sorts
With under path from pastures north to south.
Had someone copied classic arch of stone?
I'd rather think some unschooled genius here
Displayed his craft: a way to move his cows.
We tried to clear it out, my summer friends
And I, and found a hundred years and more
Of leaves and roots, stout-fingered frost, had worked
To turn our tools and thoughts to other things.

## Weather Report

The weather is sometimes what we talk about
At first, my daughter and I, on the phone
Between here and there. Today I told her what
I saw outside, "What exactly is a
Lowry day?" she asked. We see things as we
Are I guess. I had thought the whole world knew.
"A lowry day in Maine is nearly rain
And little else," I said. "Something between
A rainbow and a driving rain, what
You call your gas tank when the gauge is half
Way up—or is it, half way down?" I went
On and on with this until there came a
Sudden, "Dad, I think I get the whole idea.
You're going fishing instead of swimming."
I said, "I'm really not quite sure just yet."

*Music*

When was it Earth first heard a song?
Was it wolves howling, birds calling,
Wind moaning in corners of old caves?
All this on some vast, infinite scale,
Vibrating, filling night and day
With all the stuff of song.
And what of man? Was it mothers
Singing softly to babies, a drum
Left overnight in rain and sounding
Different from a drum still dry?
And did a people sway to the sound
And did they sing with the birds
And the wolves and the wind?
When was it Earth first heard a song?

*Ocean Eye*

Existence is the breath of soul,
Timeless as a wave-swept gem
That sparkles briefly on its uncertain
Carpet of sand, before it eases downward
Through the crystal planets,
Drifting in an hourless space
That knows no expectation,
No need for patience,
Where each new awakening
Is for the first time.

*Planting*

When I consider garden things like plants
And little trees, my thoughts loom sometimes large,
As looking back, I think I planted much
Before I knew enough to nourish well.
I got my elderberry trees today,
Four sticks with pedigrees that promise much
When planted deep enough in fertile ground.
That hardy stock comes up in spite of all
May well suffice to keep this garden strong
As I recall the years when seeds I've sowed
Flew off to garden worlds beyond my own.

*Song*

The stars hold songs that fill
   the heads and hours
Of those who wish to hear
   and put them down
So halls and hearts may feel
   the vibrancy
Of time and space and know
   a little more,
And yet, perhaps enough
   to sing with those
Whose lives and songs we knew
   and did not know—
Great universal choir,
   a part of all
There is and all there was
   that ever sang.

*Amy*

Found some footprints in the sand one day—
Wondered who had found my lonely place,
A land reserved for tides and gulls,
An island carved in ocean space.

Found a castle on the shore that day—
Placed a flag upon its highest side.
I wrote my name there in the sand
And walked away an ocean tide.

Found a name beneath my own that day—
*Amy* spelled out in the sand for me—
But when I looked for her, I saw
Her footprints leading to the sea.

Found a stone upon a mainland shore—
Saw it there because it stood alone,
And when I read the chiseled words,
I knew the sea was Amy's home.

Found a castle on the shore that day—
Was I there a hundred years ago?
We all build castles in the sand;
We build them well but they must go.

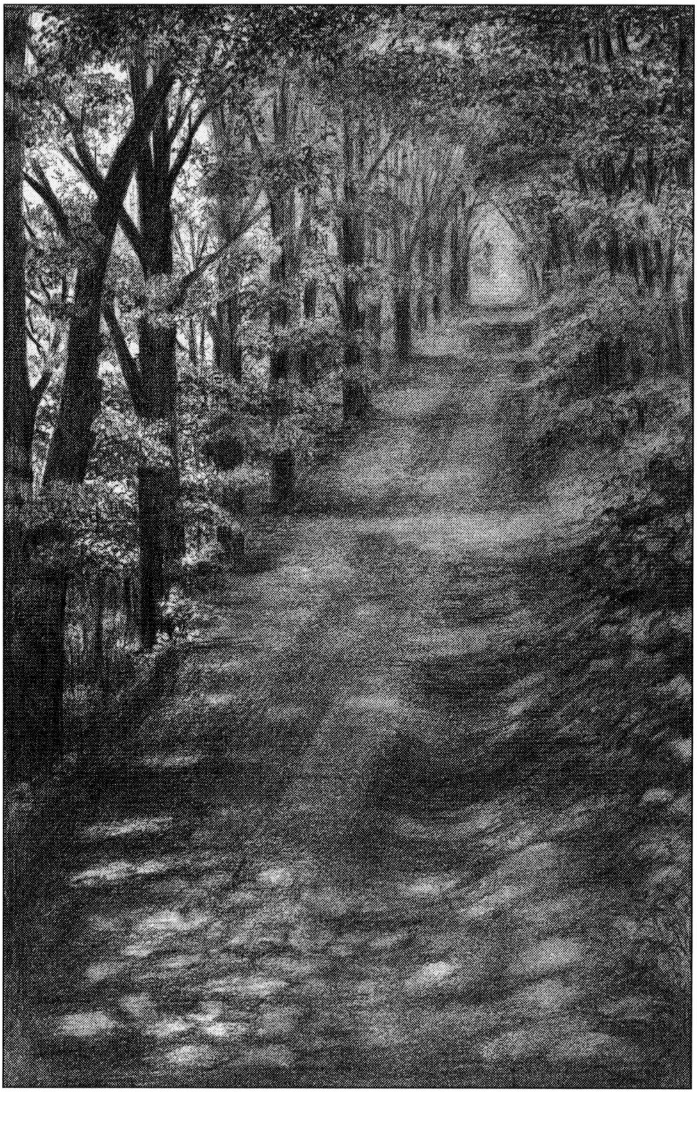

*Pathways*

The woods are full of rain
   from overnight,
And I have left my sleep
   this day to see
Soft weep of bough, new green
   of leaf, and now
A path I walked so many
   dawns ago
In woods like these I cannot
   know for sure
Where life and dreams diverge
   or where they meet
Or where I may have gone
   before my sleep.

*Smelting Time*

Half-frozen men, (whose women ponder what
It is that prompts such April lust), peer deep
Beyond the gleam that lanterns make and urge
Some ancient finny god to multiply
The pin-smelt ones and twos and bring tonight
A silver curtain sweep to current events.

*Tides*

From where I stood that day the ocean spread
To left and right beyond the dunes and, outward,
Joined the curve of earth to where it met the sky,
Then, walking downward to the sea, I heard
It pause to rest between the working of its tides—
As I must do, I thought, if I survive.
Close ahead, I saw a level dune and there
I pitched my little tent, and there I lay
In hopes a day beyond the world of man
Might, somehow, in its ocean hours, contrive
To mend the ragged canvas of my life.

I cannot say for sure if I awoke
Or stayed behind to dream, but heard a voice
In wind and wave, in whispers close enough
To make me wonder why and whence they came.
And then I found myself upon a beach
Where footsteps trailed behind me in the sand
And thence, I'm sure, to other lives and loves
All living, loving far away, still close
To heart and coming back again in dreams,
Too saddened now and not content to stay,
I left my tent but looked once more to sea
And saw a bay all hammered gold by sun,
Then walked through pink and red of border rose
And smiled once more at what was left of day.

*Early Settlement*

## Old Cellar

I found it deep in woods, a cellar hole
Made shallow by the leafy gift of fall.
A lonely place and yearly more remote,
It must have faded first within the minds
Of older folk, who saw, as in a dream,
The shuttered hope that stood for home
Ere dreamless rest erased it for all time.
Here, now, within a granite wall a scythe
Enfolds with rusted arms a tiny lump
Of faded cloth with button eyes still bright.

I had not thought that day that I might see
A part of life now far away yet close to me.

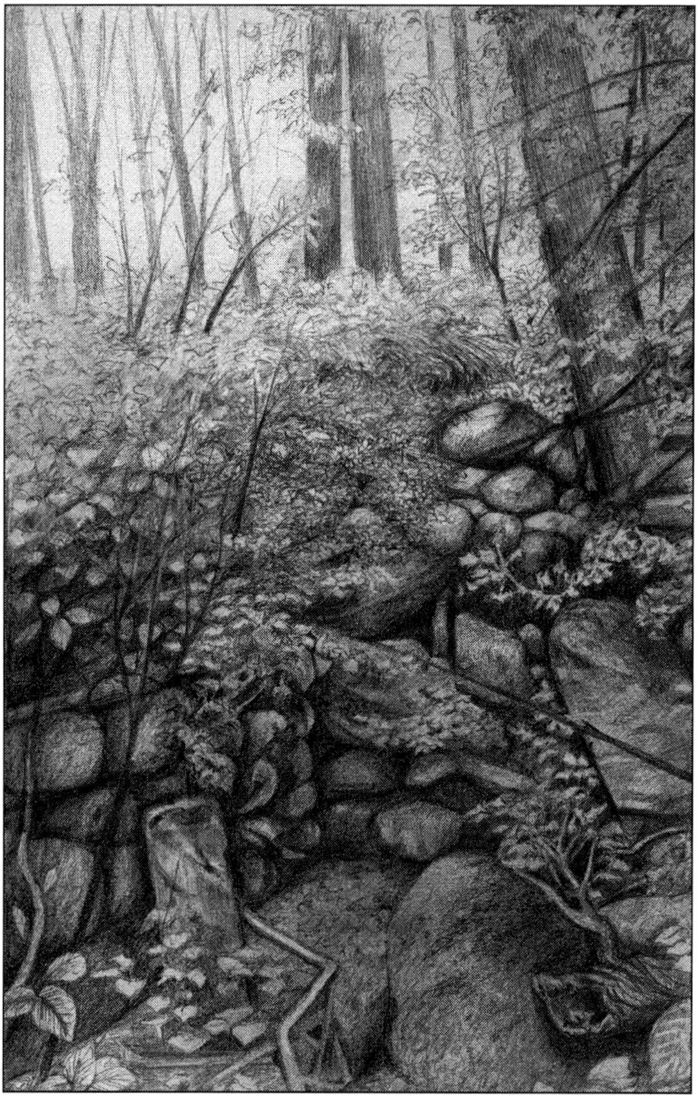

*First Settlement*

Beyond the mill, across the bridge, old roads
Meander to the farther hills, and some
Grow dim, then vanish in the shade of trees.
In younger days I walked these roads and found
Our early living place, old cellar holes
Where toes and fingers found the daily things
Of other lives beneath old autumn leaves—
Dull glass and such to fill our downtown shelves.

Off to the side of wooded lanes, old homes
Are hid and hard to see, except in spring
When scent of rose or lilac bloom lies close
To sunken stones that show the line of walls.
Here lived those whose lives turned narrow in the mold
Of all the world they knew, where neighbor's hand
Was dearest hand to hold for all of life.
The young, the old, the souls who breathed this air,
It seems they still remain to haunt us there.

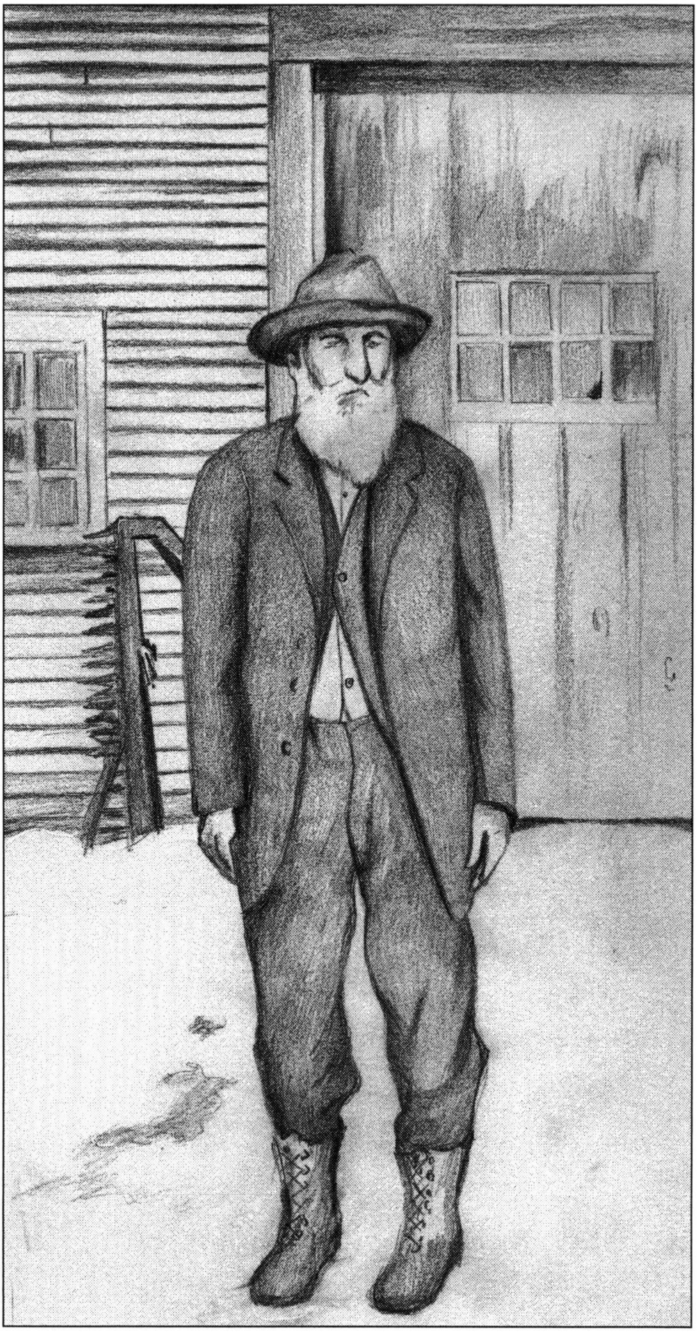

## *Ephraim*

He came alone one May and took the house
And land that Louis left when Louis left
To find another life. A drafty place
With pump and stove and sagging cot, it gave him
Shelter from the sun and rain and little else.
Before that summer passed, we think he must
Have known why Louis left. With land so scant
And soil so close to ledge, he couldn't grow
Enough to keep him through the winter months.

We saw him straining in his field and talked
Among ourselves, as neighbors often do,
And one of us with larger house and work
For all, took Ephraim in and kept him on
To work his way—a Christian board and room.
The mother of the house, as ever, mother
To them all, would view him later as she would
A father grown too old to keep his home
But having hands to help her fold her clothes
Or hold her skein when she was balling yarn.
When even that was more than he could do,
There came a dream that had no end. They gave
Him space within their family lot and chiseled
FATHER EPHRAIM on his stone and nothing more.

## *Andrew*

Andrew Edwards could not walk too far behind
The plow before it strayed to right or left,
Depending on, he said, the dreams that filled his head.
He called them *dreams* at first but soon found out
That *visions* was a better word to use
Because his folks and neighbors listened hard
At that and freed him from the errant plow.

We never called him lazy to his face,
But there were all those other tasks that went
Much harder with his help, and so we let
Him go his way and leave the work to us.
He sometimes stopped and had a word with me.
When I was only ten, he told me that
He saw strange things that never were but must
Return one day—a line of flowing white
That growled its way across a distant sky,
A man who took a snarling sword in hand
And laid a forest down within a day.
"I see such things most times I walk," he said.
"You needn't tell the rest. They'd only laugh
At me again. You know they're not like you."
We thought about the weed beside the road
That Andrew liked to chew when it grew tall
In summer time, the one we kept away
From cows and pigs, and so I never quite

Believed the things he said, but listened to them
Anyway and kept it all within my head.
"He's out too late," his sister warned one night.
Our searching took us days before we found
Him smiling in the snow below Call's Ledge.

Because the winter cold had gone too deep,
We built a box and laid him in a barn
To wait for spring, "The sooner the better,"
My father said. "Knew it all would end like this."
"He's not here," my mother said to comfort me.
But I was ten and had to know and so
I crept inside the barn sometimes to look
At him and wonder at the dream that gave
Him flight from here perhaps to other years.

## *Mary*

What sin she held was hers to see. She knew
It was her brother's child. It wasn't God's!
Her mother, if she guessed, would only curse
The narrow loft above where children slept,
Then, close of lip, go on with all her work.
And Mary, months away, took sudden walk
So deep in woods that only creatures wild
Could hear her screams, consigning all to earth
And hedgehogs come to clean the forest floor.
Back home, her mother helped her find a stove,
Then gave her what she could from what she had
To make a living place in shed out back.
And Mary nursed the sick for fifty years,
A service to man, beyond the reach of men.

## Adam

They slept not far enough apart in loft
Above, and what had started out as play
One night took on another way, when all
At once he held her down too long and found
The way to send the fourteen seasons of his seed
Too deep to suffer death. Their play was done
And with it childhood chapters closed for good.
He never knew about his little son,
But understood his sister's will to move
Out back in the room she fashioned from the shed.
Grapeshot took his legs at Gettysburg and he
Came home to know a chair and little else.
Later, when the old folks' friend, the lung disease,
Moved in to rob his strength, his sister nursed
Him through his failing light and closed his eyes.

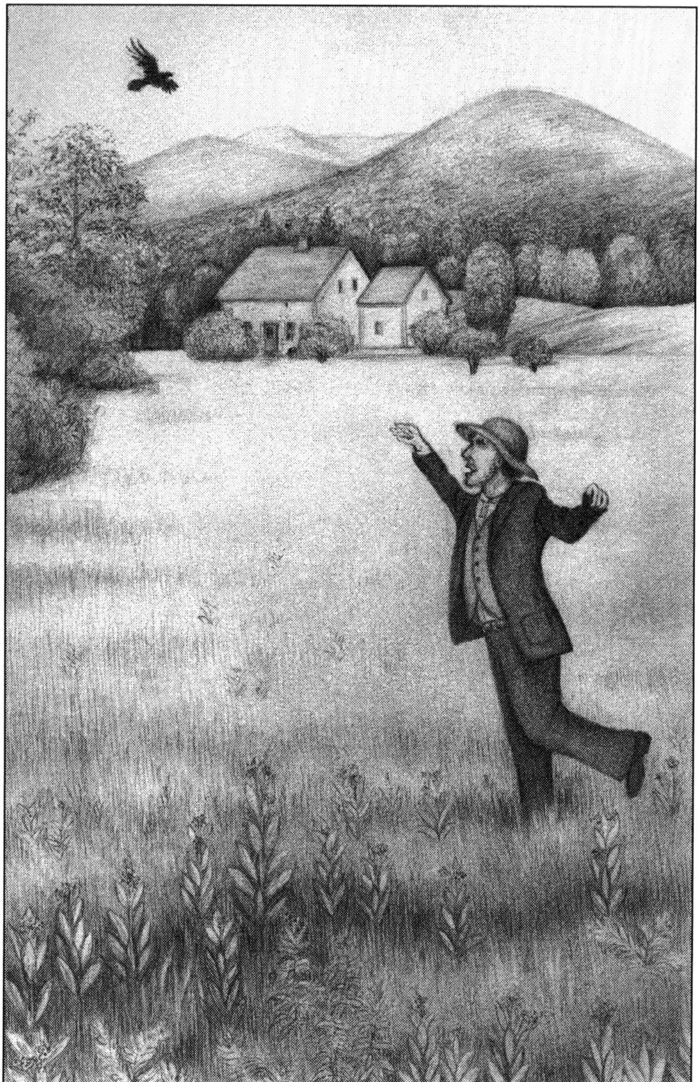

*Samuel*

The son born late to Frank and Emma Blake
Just wasn't right, we heard, and that is why
We thought they must have kept him shut away.
His baby years went by beyond our view,
And we were left to learn in other ways
Of life behind their doors and window shades.
We heard Sam learned to walk when he was three
But never learned to talk except in ways
That no one else but he and Emma knew.
His father, from away and never much
A part of local life, spent nights away
In Portland Town too many times for him
To lie and call it business any more.
At length he stayed away for good and sold
His herd and all his land, except the land
Around the house—front yard and field out back.
We sometimes waved to Sam when we went by,
But came by once to see him for ourselves.
We found him running in the field, long arms
Flapping up and down and crying like some
Baby crow too soon from nest, not yet in flight.
We thanked our God and never came again.

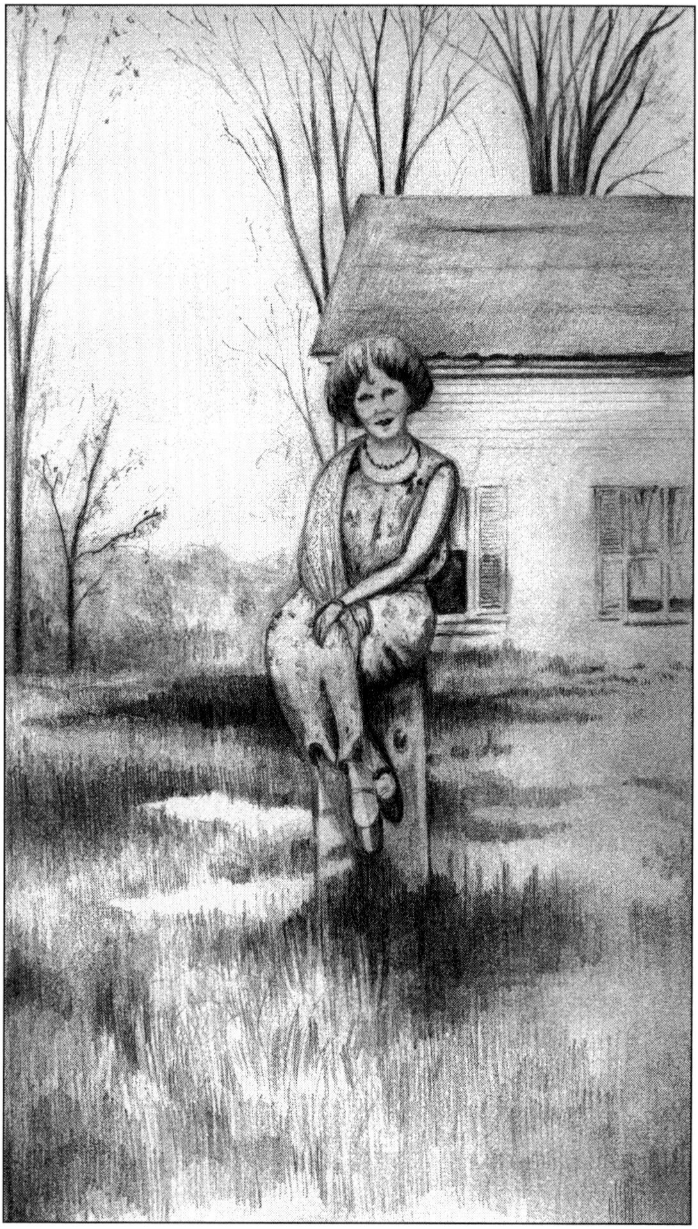

## *Clara*

A year to the day my Martha died, Fred
Brought his oldest daughter by. "Seth," he lied,
"I've come to see just how you've ditched your field
And Clara came for company." I knew
My field as hardly more than fair, when set
Against the rest of what I had, but walked
Them long enough to prompt an August thirst.
They lingered here just long enough to bring
The cider out, and while we sipped, I glanced
At her, but then I saw her look away.
I think I may have wished for her to stay,
But summer days moved on to other days.
And soon a month had passed, but then in fall
I saw her walking on my road again,
His Clara came to call on me once more.
She'd come, she said, to see the sun set on
The western hills and could I show her where
The view was best. I showed her western trees
And told her that the view of western sky
Was always best when seen from upper loft.
Then Clara laughed at me, red tongue between
Her strong white teeth, and winter senses warmed.
I think we trembled when our bodies touched
And Clara stayed and Clara stayed and stayed.

*Eunice Foss*

My husband Walter died in May, and I
Was left up there alone, alone except
For Angie Blake who lived on down the road—
Old Maid Angie with her water jug and
Crazy talk all day. My oldest son was there
And heard it all. I'd planned to move that fall
But August seemed as good a time to go.
He and Alice helped me pack and brought me here,
The town where woolen mill provides them all
Of what they need to live. They had a place
For me, a little room downstairs where I
Could sleep and sew and read. Sometimes I cook!
They say biscuits is what they all like best.
The month of June is shortcake time. Oh, I
Remember well the wilder fruit I picked
In the field behind the house. My Walter
Never mowed that field 'til picking time was done.
Oh, yes, I miss my home, and sometimes when
I go outside I see the mountain pass
That leads to maple-shaded lane and home
And barn and fields and little family lot.
We used to go and visit lilac time,
But the road got bad and Edward broke a spring.
"We'll go on up this year," they sometimes say,
But summers come and go, and I am yearly
More content to keep in dreams another life.

## Angie Blake

My neighbor had an older son in town
Who took her in, and I am left alone
To walk these empty hills and fields and lanes
And check old homes and what is left of barns.
A secret comes out bare in lonely times,
And here before her house I say there was
A day in haying time her husband asked me
For a drink, but lingered by the pump and then
Surprised my spinster skirts—and him an elder
In the church! From then 'til now the smell of
New-mown hay hangs sweeter on the hotter days
Then roses wild upon our border walls!
No longer close to hay, I sometimes pluck
A blade of grass; then holding it between
My thumbs, blow high and shrill enough to wake
The dead. And see! His grave is over there,
And she has gone and left me here with him.

## Walter

Whenever Walter Adams came to town,
He'd want to dicker, trade for what we had—
Some worldly good we'd part with for a price
He knew was lower than the price he'd get
On down the road or even here at home.
"You've got it all," we said and joked, "You'd sell
Your wife if someone offered cash enough."
"Cash enough," we said aloud, when he had gone,
"To cover for the loss of household slave."
A few years back he'd hired a girl from out
Of town to keep his house. She had his child,
A crippled boy born short of marriage vows
Who died at three from winter lung disease.
"A matter all her fault," her husband said.
"She let the fire burn down too low." We later
Learned he died devoid of pills and doctor's care.
We never saw her much except in church,
Where rouge and powder could have hid dull pain
Within her face, deep shadows in her eyes.
There came a day when Walter was in town
A better man than he came by his house
And took his wife in trade for love, then drove
With her too far away for anyone to find
A trace. (I must confess we never tried.)
And Walter never got his price for her
And died alone at home with all his things.

## Mill Town

When Dan came home, the morning moon was dim
And birds sang, it seemed to him, a newer song.
His mother from her bedroom window watched
Him walk the last few yards and turned away,
Knowing well what music lay behind a smile,
What younger yearning did to lighten steps.

At supper time their little boy, grown tall
And shoulder-broad too soon, flexed both his hands.
"The pay is good at all the mills. You rent
A place. It's what I want. I can't stay here."
"Your grandfather built *this place*," his father said.
"It'll be yours to do with what you want. I can't
Convince you home is here and what you know?"
"You know too well you can't," his mother said.
"His heart is down the hill with her and what
We have of home must be for us, not him."

He stayed to help at haying time, but when
The one last load was pitched to loft, his mother
Helped him pack his clothes, whatever else was his,
Put fingers in his hair and kissed his cheek.
"We've not seen Mary since her father moved
Away, but we know her near as well as you.
Your father? Well, he'll come to understand."

The road back home seemed long that wedding day
And Harold hardly spoke. When they stopped at the brook
To give the horse a drink, she took his hand.
"They'll come up to visit. You know they will."

"I don't think so much. He has his home with her.
You know our place is finished here with us."
She gripped his hand and made him look at her.
"They'll need us down below when babies come."
She thought of rocks and rotting sills and fields
That seemed much closer to the woods each year.
"Sometimes change is good," she said and most could feel
Their little hands on skirts and apron strings.

*Moving Day*

Their bedroom held the new half-light of dawn:
A bed not fit for two when sleep was scant,
A rocking chair by window sill, where she
Could see as far as where the road to town
Dipped down and out of sight. Behind her, arms
Outstretched, her husband snored his sleep away.
She pulled the curtain shut and left the chair.
Their spring had been a time of life-things lost—
You can't take this; you can't take that. Perhaps
They'll want the hay to feed the horse. It all
Ends today, she thought. Just leave and not look back.

Arnold stirred and blinked and quick forgot his dream
Of falling trees and new stone walls, of neighbors
Come to help him build his house and then his barn;
Of winter winds that piled the snow above
Their window sills, of burning maple, oak,
And ash to warm the souls of those inside;
Of melting frost and sudden spring and lambs
And fawns, pink bud of rose and lilac bloom,
Of summer fields of hay and sheep to shear,
Then autumn hues on hills and all the world.
He dealt with things and seldom lent his thoughts,
But now it came to him that what he had
Was never his to hold for long and so

Must be for all the world that needs to move.
So much there was to sell or give away,
So little left to use another day.

*Old Dog*

The gray of afternoon and wisping snow
From north and east proclaimed the coming storm,
And here beyond the range of human voice
He touched the bulge from broken bone and dared
Not move his leg. From where he lay he had
A clouded view of valley miles away
And tried to guess—he could not know—the hour
He would be missed, a time for bells to ring,
A time for valley men and boys to move.
They would not come in time he knew and shivered
At the thought of this, their futile search in snow
And dark at end of winter's shortest day.
Awhile the numbness came to steal his pain,
Whatever thoughts he might have had, but then
As in a dream he heard a tiny bell
And felt a gentle weight and welcome warmth
As earth and man began to slip away.

It started with his little son who left
His window seat and pulled his mother's skirt.
"He's right," her uncle said. "He's never out
This late. There's something wrong. We need to look."
He straightway rang the family bell and soon
The dooryard filled with neighbor men and boys.
"Left the heifer off at noon and should be back.

He's somewhere up the pass," the uncle said
And lit his lamp and pointed out the way.

The leading searcher's lantern found the tracks,
Huge, fresh, traversing upward in the snow.
Some said "Wolf," though wolves had not been seen for
    years,
But all could see the logic of a trail
That kept the line of path in driving storm.
They found their neighbor sleeping in a place that had
No snow, a place where tracks had come to end.
"I can't remember much of this," he said
Next day, "except I dreamt old Fred lay down
Beside me in the snow and he's been dead
For years. I have to wonder about that."

## *Reclamation*

With spring and summer, early fall all fled,
The north wind rustles first then hammers hard
On things gone by that lived on borrowed ground.
Then winter's first large storm surmounts the angles
Left by man, and family lot and cellar hole
Accept a newer silence of the snow.
Nearby white on white of boundary walls lead off
To left and right then vanish, solid food
For hungry hemlock, starving oak and pine.
Old graveyard stones seem somehow safer now,
Their earthward progress slowed in time and space
By fluff of snow, affront to gravity.
Where neighbor's lantern lights once gleamed behind
Each tiny windowpane and helped fend off
The gloom that came on winter afternoon,
An early hammock moon lends meager light,
But just enough to linger on the fur,
On hungry eyes that seek another's eyes.
A cloud and then another cloud combine
To cover up the moon, and all the earth below
Is wild again within this utter night.

CHARLES CHURCHILL was born in East Brownfield, Maine. He attended Porter schools, graduated from Fryeburg Academy, received an A.B. degree at Syracuse University, an M.A. in English at SUNY Albany and taught ten years in the capital district of New York state. He went on to teach English for twenty years at Kingswood Regional High School in Wolfeboro, New Hampshire, retiring in 1990.

Churchill lives with his golden retriever, Brandy, on Colcord Pond in Porter, Maine, where, in addition to writing, he enjoys fishing, boating, the company of old friends and community volunteering. He has four children: Susan, Gwen, Steve and Ken.

DAWN MARION has a special affinity toward the light, landscapes and people of New England that is illustrated in these graphite images. She lives in Center Ossipee, New Hampshire with her husband, Brad, and their three cats.